My World of ANIMALS™

JANELL KHU

The Rosen Publishing Group's
PowerKids Press™
New York

1

For Little Girl Sydney

Published in 2004 by The Rosen Publishing Group, Inc.
29 East 21st Street, New York, NY 10010

First Edition

Book Design: Mike Donnellan
Illustration by Mike Donnellan

Photo Credits: Cover, p. 7 © Mimi Cotter/International Stock; p. 5 © Chris Rogers/CORBIS; p. 9 photo by Mike Donnellan; p. 11 © Donna Ikenberry/Animals Animals; p. 13 © Michael Keller/CORBIS; p. 15 © Reuters NewMedia Inc./CORBIS; p. 17 © Dale C. Spartas/CORBIS; p. 19 © George Shelley/CORBIS; p. 21 © Vittoriano Rastelli/CORBIS.

Khu, Jannell
Dogs / Jannell Khu.
p. cm. — (My world of animals)
Includes bibliographical references and index.
Summary: This book introduces dogs, describing their physical characteristics, their capabilities, and their friendship.
ISBN 1-4042-2522-6 (lib.)
1. Dogs—Juvenile literature   [1. Dogs] I. Title   II. Series
SF426.5.K57 2004   2003-010265
636.7—dc21

Manufactured in the United States of America

2

CONTENTS

There are many kinds
of dogs. There are big dogs
and there are small dogs.

Dogs have fur. Dog fur
can be many colors.
Some dogs have yellow fur.
Some dogs have brown fur.

This dog has black, gray, and white fur.

A baby dog is called a puppy. Puppies grow up to be adult dogs.

A dog can be a friend
or part of a family.

Some dogs are called working dogs. This dog helps a blind person. A blind person cannot see.

Some dogs help police officers. Dogs can help police officers catch bad people. This police dog is on a leash.

This dog works with a fireman.
Dogs can help firefighters
search places that are not safe
for people to enter.

These dogs are pulling a sled. The dogs are on a mountain. Dogs make great pets and workers.

WORDS TO KNOW

leash

mountain

police officer

sled

Here are more books to read about dogs:

A Day with Your Dog
By Wes Lipschultz
Rosen Publishing

My Dog
A Book About a Special Pet
By Heather Feldman
Rosen Publishing

Due to the changing nature of Internet links, PowerKids Press has developed an online list of Web sites related to the subject of this book. This site is updated regularly. Please use this link to access the list:

www.powerkidslinks.com/mwanim/dog/

INDEX

Word Count: 142

Note to Parents, Teachers, and Librarians

PowerKids Readers are specially designed to help emergent and beginning readers build their skills in reading for information. Simple vocabulary and concepts are paired with real-life photographs or stunning, detailed images from the natural world. Readers will respond to written language by linking meaning with their own everyday experiences and observations. Sentences are short and simple, employing a basic vocabulary of sight words, as well as new words that describe objects or processes that take place in the natural world. Large type, clean design, and photographs corresponding directly to the text all help children to decipher meaning. Features such as a contents page, picture glossary, and index help children to get the most out of PowerKids Readers. They also introduce children to the basic elements of a book, which they will encounter in their future reading experiences. Lists of related books and Web sites encourage kids to explore other sources and to continue the process of learning.